True Colours

From the Universe to the Inner Mind

by

Zohra Zoberi

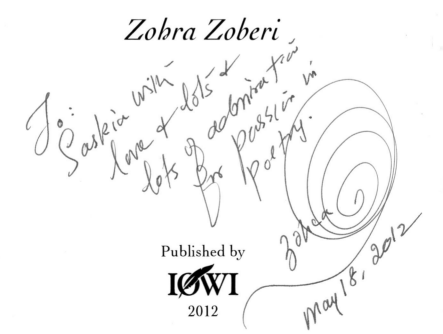

To: Saskia with
love + lots of
lots of admiration
for passion in
poetry.

Zohra

May 18, 2012

Published by

IOWI

2012

True Colours: From the Universe to the Inner Mind by Zohra Zoberi

Published by: In Our Words, Inc.
                  inourwords.ca

Cover Image &
 Author Photo: Khurram Qureshi, Digipix

Illustrator: Salim Khan

Cover &
 Book Design: Shirley Aguinaldo

Library and Archives Canada Cataloguing in Publication

Zoberi, Zohra
    True colours : from the universe to the inner mind / Zohra Zoberi.
Poems.

ISBN 978-1-926926-20-9

    I. Title.

PS8649.O24T79 2012   C811'.6   C2012-901375-7

First Printing, April 2012

PRINTED IN CANADA

Dedicated to
my lovely granddaughters

Elina
Marzia
and
Daania

Acknowledgements

First and foremost, I'd like to thank Brandon Pitts, my editor, for his keen interest and diligence in working on my book. I would also like to thank Nathan Medcalf and John Ambury of the Writers and Editors Network for their editorial comments on many of my poems. Special thanks to Salim Khan, a well-known Toronto-based artist whose illustrations not only enhance the aesthetics of this book, but the meaning of my words as well. I truly appreciate his timely accommodation of my request.

I would also like to thank my husband, Dr. Mujeeb Zoberi, for his support, love and patience, and for allowing me to bounce ideas off him, sometimes even in the middle of the night.

A special thanks to all the women I have been fortunate to have met, who have inspired me. I am honoured that they shared with me their intimate experiences of joy in love and the pain of a broken heart. Many of these poems are in fact *their poems*.

ZZ

Author's Note

There is a Persian saying *Dil ba dasth aavar ke hajj-e-akbar asth* [holding someone's heart in your hand is the greatest pilgrimage you can make]. My mother passed on the wisdom of these words to me which she had learned from her father. My heart has always been drawn to the have-nots whose stories I penned in my journals even as a teenager.

My husband's career as a researcher offered us the opportunity to travel to thirty-six countries across Africa, Asia and Europe. I feel privileged to have lived and been influenced by a wide diversity of cultures. In Canada, working as a financial planner in a bank, I very often found myself in the role of confidante and advisor with both clients and colleagues who shared personal issues with me. I was sometimes referred to as the 'therapeutic banker.' Their stories too were recorded in my journals.

I have written and produced several socio-dramas about relationship issues that have been well-received. Subsequently, many women discreetly shared their personal stories in an effort to vent their frustrations and seek comfort. On the other hand, some of my poems and stories have resonated with young women who have found in them relief for their broken hearts and a sense of empowerment and hope for the future.

My stories and poems have been published in various magazines and anthologies. Two of my award-winning plays were published in a book entitled *Questionably Ever After*, published in 2008 by IOWI.

This collection of poems is a compilation of new material as well as a selection of my favourites written over the years. I write for everyone, hence simplicity and clarity rather than ambiguity has been my style – from prose poems to poetic prose. I hope you enjoy reading them!   *ZZ   zohraz.com*

Contents

Contents [continued]

Immigrant Woman

She likely had no say
in the decision to migrate
thousands of miles
from her siblings, parents and friends
walking two steps behind
expected to tag along

But in this new climate
free from suffocation
opportunities unlimited
she put her best foot forward
walking two steps ahead

Migrating thousands of miles
did not deserve as much credit
as those four steps
she has taken on her own

Now she must struggle
to take two steps back
in order to remain in line

Against the Wind

Wearing *their* attire
carefully choosing words in *their* language
      I'm now perfectly at home
in my chosen home

Throughout lunch I listen to their stories
about the cropped ears of his dog
the forty-dollar monthly manicure for her pet
their trips to Vegas
the gambling casinos,
string bikinis they bought
healthy tans they got on the California beach

Virgin Mary, Bloody Caesar, Molson Light
they laugh heartily as they propose a toast
hesitant at first, I join them too
lift my glass of ginger ale
      comfortably at home
in my chosen home

Barbecued pork chops, liver pâté,
delicious duck, cooked in white wine
my palate accomplished
I tell myself: "boiled fish is healthy too"
      Of course I'm at home
in my chosen home

Why this exhaustion then?
Is it the pace, or the extra mile I must toil
in order to be on even ground?
I do and I dare
contribute my share,
considered to be accomplished, a mentor

I am ...
Or am I ...
at home in my chosen home?

At day's end I say my prayers
habitually flip the corner of my prayer rug
seemingly a meaningless gesture

I pause ... think ... and smile
It's what has been ingrained
I put on my *kamees shalwaar,* turn on the sitar
        I am truly at home
in my own home

Canvas of the Heart

Harsh words found a magical way
to dissipate into thin air
I smiled back

Step by step
how gradually you've descended
into the depths of my heart
reached its canvas

With gentle strokes you have enhanced
the colours of my emotional landscape
Ah, those final touches

How easy it's become
to withstand adversity

Instantly I'm able to step into my colourful world
leaving them baffled
as to why I didn't react to their sarcasm

Little do they know
I wasn't even around

True Colours

Clenched jaws ... wrinkled forehead
anger – sadness – mingled in moist eyes
bitterness pushes me forward

Standing at the top of a hill
I inhale power
Sooner or later, it has to end
we can't go on like this

Yet wandering thoughts and eager eyes
slope along green grass
smiling tulips, yellow and red
deep blue lake, light blue sky,
with hints of pink and peach
expanse of lush green ...

Bereft of colour, how dull it all would be ...

My life, a complete picture on its own
his presence, the colours in it
we have become inseparable

Longing to embrace him I return home
All is forgiven and forgotten

Valentine Dance

The theme: Love and Romance
Colour scheme: Red and White
carnations and candles – tables adorned
warm ambience, soft music
his arms lovingly encircling my waist
eyes filled with affection
as though at a signal
he would bring for me
the world of fortune

Lady in red is dancing with me ...
my favourite song played on
into a quick swirl he led me
spinning the dim lights
like the distant thoughts circling in my mind

"The most romantic couple of this evening is ...

The music suddenly stopped
drawing everyone's attention
our names were announced as the winners!

Wrapped in glitter and glow
I took the prize with a sense of guilt
our steps well-coordinated
posture perfect
seemed well-matched ... but
what happens off the floor?
Must I always dance to his tune?

Stepping down from the stage
with scepticism I shook the prize box
as though it were empty

our steps well-coordinated
posture perfect
seemed well-matched ... but

Able or Disabled

Using her arms and hands
to substitute legs and feet
she deftly climbed onto the chair
Somewhat heavy in physique
mauve dress cut down to size
she wore a bright smile

As a motivational speaker
invited to share her life story
The disability – hers at birth
challenges she had overcome
How she cooks, how she cleans
she described it all with animation
half a body, yet twice the confidence
her attitude, a priceless gem

Pity rose from the listeners
followed by wonderment
as from amidst the audience
he rose to the stage
kneeling with red roses in hand
and a gem for her finger

Disabled in appearance
to others merely half a woman
to him ... not only complete
but more than most

She smiled softly
"Yes"

Password

Willingly I gave him full access
to my personal computer, my mind
his password being my heart
folder on emotions he frequently accessed
Together we created wonderful stories
and some – not so good

Life's about downloading pleasant memories
deleting the unpleasant
I did just that

Then one day before we parted
with two simple strokes he retrieved it all
from my *Recycle Bin*
an oversight on my part
that broke my heart
why did I not think to empty the *Trash?*

Retain and retain then delete
emotions interchange
between smiles and frowns
I will have the edited version again
to cherish forever

My password, only I can protect

Dancing Birch

Sipping morning tea
relishing memories of loved ones distant
How could I resist so spontaneous an invitation
from my friendly neighbour?

No, it wasn't Cindy Lee,
in her backyard it was a young birch tree
enjoying its adolescence
coaxing me to celebrate its ecstasy
branches supple, beauty subtle

With each wave of cool breeze
soft morning sun
leaves shimmered like silver

Conversation with my soul
rose from the heart like a symphony

Sensibility enhanced
colourful birds arrived to flirt,
caress its dainty beauty, then fly away

Aroused, the birch stretched its arms in a dance
I remained in trance

Farewell to my cup of tea
I glided outside to embrace
a bright summer morning
after a long dreary winter
Pale pink petunias, bright red begonias,
the Rose of Sharon in festive mood
I strolled barefoot on the moist green carpet

Warmly greeted by those evergreens
I planted in a row
six to represent each sibling, the seventh for my mom
those of us nurtured by my father

Overcome with emotions I reached out
for that lush green, my deceased father
the solitary pine away from them all
stood firm and tall
How I would've showered them with love

Through the sprinkler a rainbow smiled
resembling siblings'
with my fingertips I could expand at will
A butterfly fluttered by
like flashbacks of our happy reunions

Puff of cool breeze patted me on the shoulder
coping mechanisms ... how creative
A glance of gratitude to the birch
I danced my way back to the house
to send a thank you card to my neighbour

Great is the love of nature

Aftermath

Unpredictable
in the aftermath
of the ruins of her romance
she leans on me
crying like a babe
with the frenzy of a toddler

Unable to catch a butterfly
she pouts like a little girl
Hormones haywire, from rebellious teenager
to grown woman, she swiftly becomes
In leaps and bounds she grows until
like a widow she mourns

Later, she approaches me with a smile
together we analyze the damage ... and
within weeks, from gloom to bloom
to her mind power I now bow

It was a meaningful chapter
her manuscript had the potential of
a masterpiece
"What's a good story without crisis," I said
yet ... she was reluctant to publish

To fight her inner turmoil
she took a retreat for a while
I had given up on her but ... surprisingly
she showed up on my doorstep again

Pilot light reignited, composure regained
"I've changed my mind: Here's the manuscript;
publish it"

Unable to catch a butterfly
she pouts like a little girl
Hormones haywire, from rebellious teenager
to grown woman, she swiftly becomes

Afghanistan Speaks

My appearance may be senile
I've become extremely fragile
Centuries old you may say
but ... even my youth was turbulent
family and friends
afflicted with this pandemic too
My children and great-grandchildren
in their struggle to survive
played with Kalashnikov guns, inherited
Ordinary toys were not their joys
girls under cosy covers were just other ploys

In search of the right path
I'm still in the dark
reluctantly holding hands with you
who might possibly have led me
in the right direction
My children may have escaped
scattered nails and planted mines
but ... how can I welcome and celebrate
your supersonic arrival?
Surely, equipment you brought
but ... the maps and directions you forgot

Devastated I am to discover
that even in the prime of your youth
you've become so blind
What has caused such a tragedy?
In this frigid cold must I wait
for yet another century
grow more decrepit
in the hope that perhaps some day
you will regain your eyesight
and insight?

The Magical Mallard

An amicable discussion
verge of an argument
stress headache imminent

For fresh air
I drove towards the riverbank
a quiet neighbourhood

Cruising along slowly, contemplating the issues
there it stood, with pride and dignity
a solitary mallard in the middle of the road

Ahead of a small bridge over a stream
it blocked my passage
that daring duck

Awestruck, I parked at a safe distance
but it wouldn't budge
Its iridescent green head, chestnut breast
white ring around the neck
grey sides and brown back
violet-blue speculum

The mallard seemed curious as though asking me:
"What are you doing here?"
I stayed still, stunned
the captivating beauty of the surroundings
soothed me

Earth's face freshly washed
air pure,
birds sang spring songs
a light drizzle created ripples upon the stream

mature willows along the riverbank
leaves pale green in spring, running down in streaks
caressing the stream

Tears of weeping willows
ironically helped me wipe mine
Absorbed in the environment
a harsh horn from behind
interrupted my daze
Uttering a soft, rasping "kreep" of complaint
the mallard took off and I ...
managed to cross the bridge

A mallard has no worries of human life
no sad emotions, no relationship rhetoric
How peaceful I'd be
if only I were a mallard too
freely I'd roam flirting with nature
I returned home, bedazzled
stress dispelled

With an urge to feed it
I went back looking for my mallard
it had already made its way to the river
but graciously, it turned around
gladly picked whatever I cast
no fuss, no complaints

If I were a mallard, I'd be deprived
of my power to reflect, ability to choose

The mallard can fly
may even walk on water
I provided it food, but it gave me
food for thought

Death of Romance

You're a unique individual
out of the norm traits I possess
so why mourn like others?

Let's just rebel against nature
celebrate the death of our romance
instead of lamenting its short-lived zest
marvel at how pragmatic we can be

Give in to our parents' apprehensions
firm convictions
fearing intercultural conflicts and confusions

"Short-term gain for long-term loss
that's what your romance would reap," they said

Isn't this why we're calling it off?
So why grieve the wisdom of our hearts?

To our final farewell
a beautiful turning point needed
our story didn't end the way we planned

Let's decorate the casket
with sweet whispers adorn and seal
the memories of our past

Aroma of Iram

Dedicated to my late friend Iram

Morning dew kissed the delicate petals
roses responded with a smile of sweet aroma
my memory of Iram, fresh as air
her gentle mannerisms, soft words
an array of colourful flowers
caressed my sensibility

Leisurely enjoying my peaceful backyard
gingerly pruning plants
gently sifting soil, inclined to reflect:

When people refrain from idle talk
seek only goodness in others
genuinely express love and affection
speak with an air of decency
like Iram, they too cast
the aroma of goodness
in the garden of life

The fragrance she left behind
an everlasting inspiration

Friendship

To my friend Sadiqa

Opposite ends of a precious chain
far apart and yet well linked
wrapped in a velvet pouch
tucked away inside my jewellery box

Once in a blue moon
when this chain is worn
the two ends are so well-clasped
this bond is stronger than
all other links

Cannibals

Gleefully
they cut her into pieces
and delightedly devoured

Appetites sated
fat bellies burped
and belched out
all their insecurities

A backbiting session thus ended

By the Seashore

If life were comprised
of just a few days
     seasons lasted but a few hours
spring, summer and fall
spells of sunshine disrupted by sporadic rain
followed by short-lived thunder
     and then ... calm
I would seize each and every moment to its fullest
     Or would I?

Along the seashore I walk holding hands
with my inner thoughts—my intimate friends
     Waves surging
like desires from within
one after another
breaking upon the shore
like my fantasies before fully evolving
again and again in constant retreat

In the heat of the moment
blazing sun looks down upon me
as I walk along with my feet barely wet

Clothed in my inhibitions, apprehensive
reluctant to take a plunge
into the ocean of spontaneous pleasures
     But why?

At least I've made it to the seashore
what a cooling effect the wet sand has
as the waves retreat
     Though I seem to be losing sand underneath

I try not to wobble
despite the undercurrent
I continue my journey, undaunted

      Is it all about consolation ... or
           wisdom of the heart?

*Along the seashore I walk holding hands
with my inner thoughts—my intimate friends*

Marriage

Much the same
as our relationship with food

Initially we may revel
in gourmet meals, exquisite cuisine
anticipation, preparation in advance
candlelight and romance
fancy accessories

For variety
even splurge on junk food as a treat

As time goes on we realize
fat is bad for cholesterol
sugar we have to limit
Then one day the doctor tells us
blood pressure must be controlled
avoid salt, reduce spices
stick to fat-free diet

It may become boring
but we learn to live with it
Long-term benefits outweigh
short-term pleasures

Acceptance arrives ... reluctantly
taste develops ... eventually
allowed to cheat ... rarely

To give ourselves a treat
add a little butter, sprinkle some salt
     Still
it's worth the price we pay
for sensible eating they say
leads to a healthier life

Car Wash Epiphany

Dedicated to the victims of the Iraq War

As I handed over my keys
two muscular youths instantly rushed
with powerful machines they sucked out
each and every particle of dirt and dust

Perfectly aligned to the black track
the wheels automatically rolled on
Protected against outside elements
inside a glass corridor I walked along
watching this prize possession of mine
to witness how it was being pampered
      my metal child!
What about the children of flesh and blood?

Images of disaster in a faraway land
rolling in the reel of my mind, I could see
a desperate mother begging for a glass of water
let alone afford the luxury to bathe her infant
as gallons and gallons of water gushed out
from all directions
washing the exterior till it sparkled

I walked along keeping pace
A flashing sign lit up,
"Turtle wax now being applied"
Haunted with the war images
of shelling and carpet bombing
Pure white suds softly landed all over my metal child
big brushes automatically jutted out
moving in circles
gently caressed its body
until the hubs of the wheels shone

More water gushed forth
for the final rinse
In "Shock and Awe" I stood still
More robust teens with cheery smiles
rush to grab this baby with pleasure
time to towel dry
Seeing pure white towels I couldn't help thinking
about hospitals devoid of bandages,
innocents injured with no medicine
haunting me still
the hazel eyes of a maimed teenager
his entire family lost in war

Soon they handed me the keys
Like everyone else
I too accelerated and
merged into an ever-flowing stream of steel
guzzling away the fluid that kept us moving
A blessing for some
a curse for others

I too moved on
into the daily mundane
as if
nothing had happened

The Dawn

At times, your friendship
was an island in a troubled sea
other times,
merely a mirage in the desert
Clichés I've lived through and survived

I couldn't keep chasing forever
composure I've attained
time has arrived
for *you* to come along
wherever I happen to be

Witnessing dawn's beauty
taking place
it's dawned on me,
        the thought of you
should glow inside my heart
like the dawn before my eyes

Breast Cancer

I finally summoned the courage
faced the mirror and broke down
life smudged
that deadly revelation
devastation

In a matter of days
my femininity ruthlessly mutilated
how coldly they declared
"We have removed as much as we could"
And now I had to suffer the aftermath

How lovingly you used to run your fingers through
my long hair that is no more
Apprehension ran through my emotional veins:
Will you be as scared at the sight of me
as I am?
Love me the same way you did before?

Just when I felt the woman in me had died
you whispered to me:
"My love is unconditional. I love you for you"

So expressive, for the first time
Though I felt mutilated
you made me feel complete
thank you darling

 Platonic Love

Nurtured over the years
this beautiful bond
free from the worries of grocery bills
pots, pans, and *Fantastic Bleach*

Meeting of the two minds
sharing and caring hearts
free in spirit and creative
a rare blessing
to be captured and cherished

You've finally cemented the bond
only to discover
you may be reading the same book
but never on the same page
while you're trying to absorb the chapter on *Trust*
he is still stuck on *Lust*

Multi-Tasking

To Marilyn

Multi-tasking with great intensity
how exhilarating for our brains

Programmed to perform
at times I press the enter key twice
too slow for my taste, that computer of mine

Sixty seconds in front of a microwave?
far too long to wait
I run along to achieve
yet another task in the meantime
a split of a second
has finally become virtual

Boredom with wrong channels
no longer my problem
empowered with the remote I control sixty stations
faster is better, acceleration amazing
fast food; quick copy; instant banking;
time is money

The needle set at one-hundred-twenty
my hand on the wheel
shoulder twisted to hold my cell,
in communication I am in command

It's all about technology
What about biology?

Roses are ignored, fireplaces abandoned
pine nuts ... somewhat stale

Half of me is running the rapid race
the other half being pulled back with full force
is my body evolving too?

Desire, need, culture, emotions
what's being gained and
what's being lost?

Just a Game

A seed of love flourishing in my womb
I grew physically, spiritually
with dreams and aspirations for my child –
tomorrow's man

Sounds of soldiers' footsteps
escalating by the second
I could no longer escape
vultures excited at the sight of prey

"Is it a girl, or a boy?"
They made their bets, undid their zippers
shrill voices, repulsive laughter
Extreme circumstances numbed me so
I could no longer feel pain

Naked I lay, bathed in blood
my belly slit
foetus set on fire, right before my eyes
my heart ceased to beat
Their empty bottles left behind

Ironically, no one felt the need to divulge
the faith of either the victim
or the perpetrators

In the heart of Europe
dreams defiled
Bosnia desecrated

Forest Fire

When widespread flames
rage through vast woodlands
it's devastating
be it India, Australia, or California

Panic strikes!
Emergency declared!
It becomes headline news

Media reports spread like wildfire

Street after street
row after row
as I drive through my neighbourhood
on a garbage day
blue boxes and grey boxes
waste paper spilling over
fancy brochures and pamphlets unread
free newspapers sometimes unopened
elastic bands still wrapped around them

Do I protest?
Create panic?
Make the headline news?

The forest is on fire, every single day

Survival

Amidst a grove of green
one tree stood unique
half its barren branches burnt black
the other half bursting with vitality
the contrast enhances its beauty
the trunk firm, roots strong

What caused such trauma?
What feeds this thriving?

Of the entire forest, that one tree
an unforgettable impression
stirs emotions

Somehow it resonates
in our reality

What caused such trauma?
What feeds this thriving?

2K Bug

Brilliant minds hard at work
at the turn of the century
to save our world from potential disaster
a two digit error, the Y2K Bug

For once our global village united
one common objective
I was excited

What about all the other "bugs?"
humanity faces
Hopeful, I too set out to prepare my list
I watched the news:

a woman in a coma for ten years

How did she get pregnant?

In the heart of Europe
a ten-year-old made to dig his mother's grave

Who shot his family before his eyes?

Mass graves, gang rapes
A sweet sixteen turned into a sex slave

Who buried her behind a brick wall?

A shooting rampage in a school

How does a mother bid farewell to her child?

Babies with potbellies suffer the hunger

To the lovers of soap opera,
it's all entertainment

Brilliant minds, still obsessed
united and focused on Y2K
the deadline within sight
anxiety mounted

I watched the elite around the conference table
discussing matters of great importance
such as the "Blue Dress"
Human progress at its peak

They boast about the age of technology
how far we've come!
For the political dilemmas ...
"Let's find military solutions!"

As the clock was ticking for the turn of the century
one big mistake they were ready to admit
their only blunder
frantically fixing the two digit error

As the entire world joined hands
I wondered,
Can we set a new deadline
to fix one by one
our human blunders
not just two digit errors?

The hour finally struck
fireworks lit up the skies
millions gathered at St. Peter's Square
The Eiffel Tower sparkled in my eyes
Big Ben played, *Sweet dreams are made of these...*
irony in the air

The CN Tower in Toronto,
Times Square in New York
one by one as the colourful galaxies unravelled
from one end of the globe to the other
songs of harmony gave me hope

Without a glitch we did it!

With my own list of 'bugs'
eager to return to our global village
I landed on earth
but with a thud

Creative Evaporation

I may come across as ignorant
so what?

I only enter the world of objective reality
once in a while, as a necessity

In the realm of subjective reality I thrive
at least there's room to manoeuvre

Perhaps my left temporal is in motion
for I can feel a vast realm of creativity inviting

Far more exciting is the spiritual journey
however distant the destination

Probing into scientific humdrum
solid proofs of this, that, and the other
don't seem to excite me much

I'd rather remain fluid, continue to flow
to eventually merge
or simply evaporate

There's a Room for You

To Reva and Brian

In the replica
of our global village
there's a special room
where east meets west
north greets south
and light dispels darkness

Through the mysterious corridor
you spiral
down the dark stairway
to descend in order to
'ascend'

On the one end
a large *deevan*
comfy *gao-takiyaas*, silk cushions
with paisleys and peacocks
banarsi organza drapes a stage
where musicians play happy melodies
poets recite verses, in English and Urdu

A hand-crafted copper lamp, tall and majestic
soft light glowing through
intricate filigree design
creates a romantic ambience
which candlelights enhance

On the opposite end the look is 'western'
a sofa, tables and chairs
royal blue and apple green
bring it all together

A hand-printed prayer in Arabic calligraphy
"Oh Giver of Life, the Sustainer of Life,
Bless us with all your Mercy"
how it's reflection in the mirror
hugs the opposite wall

Moderately decorated
this "exclusive" venue is inclusive
of all races
multi-coloured faces
ordinary people perform
extraordinary deeds
a symbol of harmony
no stereotyping
true bonding
interracial, interfaith and intercultural
people from all walks of life converge
creativity for a common cause:
"Enlightenment through entertainment"

In the past
socio-dramas rehearsed
social issues debated
complexities of relationships

While identifying issues
commonalities discovered
diversity celebrated
gaps bridged
seeking common Canadian values

The magic of our multicultural mosaic
truly sparked when;
Eyal of Israel and *Gada* of Palestine
held hands and bonded
Indian *Reena* played Pakistani *Zarina*

people in *sarees, sarongs* and *kimonos*
mingled with those in skirts and blue jeans
United Nations truly 'united'

How we relished those lunches
of *Shami kebab,* Italian Pizza, *Szechwan noodles*
sushi, perogies and *falafal*
a potluck of food and folk

This 'Replica' differs from
our outside world we may proudly say:
complete harmony exists!
This is a room
where you bring your basket full
empty it and refill
till it overflows

No matter what colour you are
tears are all the same
laughter alike
The *I* less significant
us matters
and there is room for *you*

It all started with
just a basement in my home

Dry Flowers

Gazing at a bed of pink, peach and red roses
I felt hollow inside
today we had said goodbye

When in full bloom
our love was once like those flowers
filled with colour and life

How we made promises to be that way forever
forgetting that the roses too will be parched one day
just as our love seems to have dried

Looking at my neighbour's garden
I sadly exclaimed, "All your flowers have died!"

"Oh, but the wise man always prepares another
bed,"
he said while planting new seeds

At the end of the veranda stood his charming wife
arranging dry flowers in a vase

Pointing towards pink roses
carefully pinned on the line to be dried
not to lose their shape and beauty
she wittily responded:
"And the wise woman preserves and cherishes
even the dry flowers"

The Deserving Hands

Poor in pursuit
I've been rich in restraint
but now ... my heart is in my hands

What have these two little hands not done?
Caught ladybugs when I was a child
folded papers into boats and birds
helped me write exams in my youth

Then with just a few simple strokes
signed my life into the hands of another
to be adorned with painted nails and diamond rings

Within the four walls of this Cinderella's castle
no stone was left unturned
these hands mopped floors, cleaned toilets
massaged feet of loved ones
with skilful strokes of fingertips
transformed fabrics into garments
planted flowers, frozen fingers even shovelled snow

Oh! Those pots and pans and Mr. Clean on my hands

These little 'gadgets' have bandaged wounds
patted shoulders
counted pennies in tough times
clenched into tight fists to curb anger
then lifted themselves into prayers

Such skills these hands willingly acquired
to be shaken with total strangers
in a manner that would clinch business deals
often more profitable to others!

The same two hands helped me win
medals for all the games I've played
of fidelity too

These fingertips
captured moments of pleasure and pain
through poetry, plays and painted portraits

All the while in toil
through tasks interesting or chores boring
music in the background
for these hands added aesthetics to my own dance
and to the dance of life

But now, when the music plays
these hands have a nagging craving;
they tap to the rhythm,
yearn for another pair of hands in tune
to tap along with
to gently hold them

Hands that will not strike, constrain
or just lift them on a pedestal
hands that will even appreciate
the scars and wrinkles
make the destiny lines sparkle

Is it just a fantasy?

My heart is now in my hands
but the butterflies ...
perhaps out of reach

A Discarded Story

Like a child after a scary dream
looking to parents for protection
she entered our clinic

"May I see your health card please?" I asked
"What's that?" she meekly mumbled
"Your date of birth?"
"I can't remember," she whispered
I helped her take off her fluffy mink
she was dressed in baby pink
the desire to keep up appearances evident
though her back was bent with osteoporosis
Eyes hollow, wrinkled face
fear seemed to rush through her bulging veins
"Isn't there someone to take care of you?"
"I don't know, p... p... perhaps there was," she stuttered

If she were to pass away
several loved ones might suddenly emerge
claiming to be near and dear
But where are they today?
Can no one accompany the vulnerable soul
for a visit to her doctor?

I saw her turn and tremble
like a piece of paper with mistakes
torn from a book, rolled up and cast into the waste

I picked up that piece of paper
inscribed with a tale of wisdom

Dandelions

Dandelions this spring
have sprung with full swing
A dear friend had bid farewell
as last winter had just set in
in the depth of my heart I shivered
How soon can feelings take another turn?
Like the weather has its mood-swings

Trees saddened, twigs dried
every vein of my emotions parched
realization of the inevitable was – "inevitable"
the death of a long-lasting romance
fluffy snow melted then froze into icicles too
I accepted it all with a shiver or two

But ... since *you* have come into my life
the memory of that dreary winter is finally fading;
fresh twigs have suddenly reappeared

The onset of a new romance
is like the arrival of another spring
once again my heart wants to sing
fresh lyrics it automatically brings
the old music switched off
flowers brighter, fragrance finer
sunshine warmer, pastures greener

Casting bright yellow smiles
randomly scattered, these dandelions tell me:
"We don't have to follow the rules of the garden,
only the good news we're here to bring"

Inside my heart
the excitement has sprung full swing

Internal Flame

Candle of romance
silently burns
illumination of emotions
an aura aromatic
music of the soul
soft and soothing

At times, the flame flickers
settles into an upward streak
smoke in serenity fascinating

Once it reaches the inevitable
the turbulent tremble of the flame
puts itself out

It's best to wipe off the remnants
let the hidden spot cool down
it must breathe fresh air
allow time before lighting
yet another candle of romance

Keep the internal flame eternal

At times, the flame flickers
settles into an upward streak
smoke in serenity so fascinating

The Intrepid

In my grey *Prism* I travelled
in the slow lane – tense
Raindrops attacked my windshield
each swipe seemed to invite more
highway unfamiliar – blurry, inside and out

In your black *Intrepid*
out of the blue you reappeared
slowed down and signalled me
On the exit ramp, you pulled out a map
highlighted in yellow, the route for me
our destination – the same

Energized, I merged into the fast lane
the rain stopped; all was clear
deep blue sky, floating white clouds
side by side we drove, exchanging smiles
When suddenly you took an unexpected turn
without any signal or wave goodbye

So, why was I so shocked?
It wasn't the first time
Swift thoughts flashed
like the blinking break lights
a near hit I missed

With fresh determination
I pressed the accelerator tempted to speed
but – better judgment prevailed
I set my cruise control
Fully confident, I zoomed along
towards a different direction altogether
with a witty smirk and a sigh of relief
The 'intrepid'

Twin Towers

Awestruck, shivering
I shrivelled into my sofa
tears rolled down to my neck as I watched in disbelief
panic-stricken executives running for survival
raging police cars, speeding ambulances
The ominous ugly cloud that choked
all of humanity
Oh God! Let this not be the work of the people of my faith
which taught me nothing but love and peace

Night after night,
to the challenge of insomnia I rose
my fingers nervously flipping channels
if only I had the power to change
the channel of violence that escalated
I beseeched: *Allah, Khuda, Yahweh, Bhagwaan*
are you not one and the same?
Can you hear me lament in the middle of the night?
I cried for the American mother
whose son vanished in the towering inferno
I could feel the pain for the Afghan woman
suffocating in her *burkha*
I also wept for the young minds being purchased
in exchange for a few morsels
In vain were my laments

Destruction and counter-destruction
the 'new world order'
repercussions lingered, of yet another war
images across the ocean
of innocent children
dodging weapons from above

Lost for answers, in my restlessness
I would travel back in time
to reflect upon the day
I had said goodbye to my loved ones
thousands of miles away
Just one suitcase, a few jewels of a newlywed
fistful of strong values from the east
the prized possessions I had brought along

The initial days I would sadly recall
lonely Christmas holidays spent
secretly sobbing
envying the family gatherings of my colleagues
in the new homeland I had chosen
Unable to attend my brother's wedding
or my father's surgery
but despite all
adept to adopt and adapt
I remained adamant, continued to weigh the tradeoffs
soon I had blended in, I was happy, proud

Three decades of training myself
and my offspring
passing on to him the moral values
from the two cultures
best of both worlds, east and west
a fine process of combining
retaining, rejecting, and upholding
that balancing act I so enjoyed
Shared stories of Prophets Mohammed, Moses, Jesus
visited Gurduaras with my Sikh friends
attended Jewish and Buddhist ceremonies
celebrated Hindu Divali festivals
learned to sing Christmas carols
with such abundant joy

On that morning
my dream of a unified peaceful coexistence
– shattered
Yet another ugly turn by humans
the stereotyping hard to escape
misunderstandings would compound
What about millions of peace-loving people
I speak for?
what about *my* twin towers of values
that took decades to build?
The torch my parents passed on to me since age three
so vividly imprinted on my mind,
the story of our Prophet,
how someone tossed garbage upon him daily as he passed by
but the day she chose to refrain, out of concern he stopped
to check the well-being of his offender
Now he is depicted and defamed through cartoons?

When the clock turned 9:15 on that ominous day
it wasn't only precious lives lost
a faith was hijacked, humanity swindled
A small brown chip, how could one separate me
from this colourful mosaic?

Confined to living room whispers
our apprehensions and fears concealed
who defines "We" and "They" and why?
Aren't we all human beings?
In the interest of humanity
we must safeguard ourselves
– *together*

Anticipation

My eyes are paintbrushes
only swifter a thousand times
The window in front, a frame
around the canvas of the outside view

In bright yellow I paint a maple first
through which slides a squirrel black
an evergreen spruce neatly trimmed
creating contrast in colour and form

A few clouds here and there
making magic in my eyes
orange branches of a nearby maple
dance with the breeze
gladly shed a few more leaves

Down the tree another squirrel
playfully rustles through the multi-coloured carpet
inviting attention to the fallen leaves

My painting suddenly becomes dim
then instantly bright as the clouds move on
With only a few swift strokes
commences the shimmering golden rain again
and I wonder
would the aging process be as beautiful?

Editing Myself

Line by line
cultural conditioning written in black
religious restrictions firmly bind
create moral dilemmas
only the craving heart is
in harmony with deep desires

The adamant mind with its inhibitions
in conflict and combat with fragile emotions
What's right? What's wrong?
Who will be the judge, and why?
The temptation of a lifetime
should I really let the moment slip away
could you possibly give me all I wanted

Desire protests, reasoning pacifies
I delete the *Yes* and retain a *No*
Editing myself at this stage
is like deleting a beautiful chapter of my life
before I begin to write it
Perhaps it's in *our* best interest

Isn't life but a first draft?
We edit as we go along

Organ Trade

Third World organs of less precious beings
mysteriously make their way
into First World bodies
However ugly this trade may be
with physical removal,
bloody scalpels and scarred bodies
at least some lives are saved

Much more destructive is the abstract form;
mass trade of the organ
of which no physical removal is needed
Brilliant minds of the have-nots
masterminded, purchased and bundled in bulk
for next to nothing
in exchange for food and shelter
"Brain contamination" colourfully called:
"Brainwashing"
What deadly destruction of humanity

Traders in this business
from the Third World and the First
are well disguised

Emotional Block

In anticipation of the expected encounter
ideas accumulated
phrases formulated
my internal monologue continues
to be translated into a dialogue
perhaps?

As the hour approaches
such a mysterious spell is cast
the resolve dissolves;
chain of thoughts disconnects
key words stumble
unnecessary details fumble

Patiently you listen
as if trying to seek answers
pretending not to comprehend
even though you do
While I suffer from stage fright
like an actor
I may well have rehearsed my lines
but once again all you get
is between the lines

Soon, we depart and
I return to the same old routine
to reformulate
rehearse all over again
only in vain

Istakhaara

A special prayer in Arabic – before making a tough decision

From a language, we usually borrow
controversial words only
why not adopt
some valuable expressions for a change?

For the dilemmas difficult and
confusions hard to handle,
let's add positive terms
to the universal dictionary of 'human solutions'

When the 'no' gets submerged into a 'yes'
the yes has a hard time staying afloat
persistent mind and heart begin to dilly dally
logic loses power
temptation tests resistance
Let the mind list its cons
feel the pulse of your heart's pros

Meditate, say a prayer, and
consult a higher authority – if you have one
or draw from Cosmic Energy
then cuddle over the muddle before falling asleep

Once you wake up
the 'combined wisdom' will often descend:
Neither just in your heart, nor just in your mind
Call it a gut feeling or sixth sense
the process you adopted is *'Istakhaara'*

This Divine Wisdom comes
with one condition though
the resolution is *final*
there's no looking back

Dewdrops

Gently place the hand of your caring nature
on the shoulder of my spiritual sensuous being
like dewdrops upon a rose petal
you'll feel my fragrance enhance
in response

Life is too short

Joe's Garden

In twists and twirls
he trimmed his trees and twigs
into perfect shapes and forms
day in and day out
tirelessly he toiled
Every now and then he would stand afar
glance with pride and praise
his own creation

From across the fence I often watched with envy
how green was his grass compared to mine
for some reason his trees bore more fruit
the colours of his flowers
much more vivid than mine
ostensibly so
forever fresh were his evergreens too

Overlooking from my upstairs window
I couldn't help notice
a bed of roses in his backyard
remained permanently parched
Had Joe no time to nurture it
had he inadvertently forgotten about it
or perhaps given up trying to even revive it?

Suddenly one day
his wife Maria stepped outside
and placed a sign
'For Sale' written in red
His lonely child was crying outside
Joe had finally left his home
in search of a new rosebud

Now I find, I must mind
my own business
mend my fences, water the yard
to keep my own pastures green

Fragrance of Joy

With childlike excitement I opened the door
to receive my bouquet of flowers
every nook and corner of my empty home
suddenly filled with the fragrance
of innocent beauty
and colourful joy

Symphony of love and affection
rising in my heart
amidst exchanges of smiles
clicking cameras
flashing lights
I tried to preserve as much as I could
for it to last as long as possible

Hours turned into minutes
minutes flew by in seconds
Once again, my house is empty
I'm hoping that the fragrance of this joy
will last until the next visit
by my children's children

The Eternal Child

Infatuation of younger years
unspoken
no wishful expectations, no disappointments
nor aging to be endured
Like a precious pearl intact inside its shell
submerged in the mysterious depths
of an ocean unknown, the subconscious
Mind and heart in a deep romantic combine

Love at the age of maturity by contrast
a complete journey of fulfilment
Powerful, frequent, fragrant
moments of ecstasy in the *"happily ever after"* ... but...
as the cycle of mundane keeps rolling
"for granted" somehow paves its way
Fragile through aging, love's limbs may even limp
hurdles at times harder to overcome
What if
craving for *"once upon a time"* sometimes takes hold?

Unexpectedly emerges from the ocean
the eternal child that never grows old
Through intricate memory lanes
it comes to rescue
Tensions eased, inner being starts smiling
how wisdom flirts with simplicity
as if an innocent child is helping the old man
cross the bridge once again

The child then submerges and
the two shadows slowly disappear
into the evening light of the golden forest
Mature love – unchanged

The child then submerges and
the two shadows slowly disappear
into the evening light of the golden forest

Fear of the Unknown

With a massive jolt
a major fault occurred
our world split in two

Gravity pulls me
to the half where I don't wish to be
the other half reluctant to rescue

Clinging to the cliff, I'm dangling in the air
the depth of this crevasse is unknown

Fear of flying, fear of dying, of aging
losing a loved one or even one's job
all too familiar

What most of 'the other half' are oblivious of
is the new form, secretly spreading fast

Overshadowed by a few filled with hate
are millions of peace-loving people
living in constant paranoia, "what's next?"

Their faith, hijacked by some, stereotyped by others
residing in the media's blind spot
is now a nation of its own
alienated
misunderstood, and out of the picture

Of their plight, others may continue
to turn a blind eye, or a cold heart

Simple Words

New words she's just learned
my granddaughter only two
"because" and "of course"
so fascinating, from a tender mouth
uttered in appropriate context too
How did she grasp these concepts? I marvelled
each time I'd give her a hug and a kiss
with pride and delight

"Because" and "of course"
ostensibly simple
their complications to an adult,
ample
Many words she'll continue to learn
the older she grows
the more difficult they may become
It's taken *me* decades to conclude:
my "of courses" should never be
reflections of submission;
of confidence and determination instead
and my "becauses" won't be excuses,
only justifiable justifications

Lessons for her I'll save for the future
for now just relish
the spontaneity with which
she keeps repeating
rehearsing
over and over
those simple words

Golden Journey

Complexity
of psycho-neuro-endocrinology
raging emotions
heated exhaustion
hypothalamus deprived, estrogens depleted
happy today, sad tomorrow
medication ... or meditation?

How one thing leads to another;
accepting physical changes aside
the desire to get in touch with my inner self,
spirituality
emotional well being
took such a strong hold
nature cooperated

Tango, waltz, cha-cha-cha
ego finally exhausted all its dances
Although a series of stones were cast
causing ripples in the water
the lake of my existence finally calmed down

No longer do I feel
the desire to compete
or worry much about outer appearance
Conscious effort reaped its benefits
superficial friendships
frivolous connections
lost importance

Surrounded by those who accept me
love me for who I am, not what I possess
I'm content

Their smiles like rainbows after a storm
colours more vivid
enhanced are the melodies of my favourite songs
endorphins are dancing with sheer delight
the entire universe seems in harmony again
into it I float,
on my designated path
with relative ease

Unfolding the glittering gift of insight
shimmering on the inside
I look forward to my golden years

Harassment

Fast asleep, peacefully she is lying in my bed
gently I caress her soft, silky hands
dimples at the back of her tiny little fingers
how vulnerable she can be

Emotionally bruised
from an unexpected encounter
A man of such dignity and honour
what high regard I had for him
Of my vulnerability
he assumed he could take advantage

Mountain of respect he bulldozed
attempted to unbutton my blouse
bullying into my dignity and honour
instantly stripping himself of decency
Forceful attempt to attack my emotions
repulsive were his hands
ugly became his face

For comfort I look to my side
holding her hand in mine, I caress
reflecting upon the incident over and over
seeking refuge

I look at her face again
she encompasses such serenity
innocence enviable
I caress her milky hands
skin so soft
she's still fast asleep
I hope and pray for her
never to be subjected
to the horror I experienced

The reel of time rewound
ever since I was a young girl
just like her
memories of other harassments surfaced
from childhood
through adolescence ... but
he was the most repulsive of all those creeps
would not take 'no' for an answer

How I had cherished his friendship
my family's trust he had earned
What a strong bond we had developed
entangled are our social connections
inter-dependent are our ambitions
A great deal must be severed now
but how?

In the dim night light
she opens her big beautiful eyes
looks at me, still wide awake
draws comfort
secures my presence by placing
her tiny leg on mine
to fall asleep again

Her innocent breathing, sweet and aromatic
in contrast to that creep's
deep breathing, so repulsive I can't forget
ugly attempts to convince and lure
spitting out blatant assumptions
compliments 'insulting'

Should I have punched him in the gut
slapped him in the face
pushed him out of the house
or simply called the police?

What do you do to such a close friend?
How can a man of such dignity
let his animal instincts turn so ugly?

Doesn't he know
it takes two consenting adults
to make an encounter legitimate?
Delicate emotions can never be overpowered
by physical strength
persuasion by force
works the opposite way

Sincere friendship badly bruised
as I recall over and over
pornographic fantasies he whispered

Relieved after such a narrow escape
I know I'll soon overcome
but still wonder,
how to shut him out off my life
will forgiveness ever be part of this scenario?
Will I eventually understand and empathize
that he may be lonely
starved for affection
a product of a society dysfunctional
that shaped him so?
Could such an ill-attraction
ever be sincere at its root?

Still battling insomnia
I hold her close again and pray
that *she* never has to go through
sexual harassment
For now we all protect her but
for the rest of her life
she'll have to safeguard herself

A Hungry Mouse

Through the back door it sneaked in
energetic youngsters excited
to find thrill in the chase
Constant feeding, rapid multiplication
soon there were mice here, there, and everywhere
floor to floor and room to room
The executives in Dior shirts, Calvin Klein ties
looked down to witness the chase
From posh offices of skyscrapers they planned
their instant escapes from the rat race
with touchtone phones they dialled
to order their jets for holiday resorts
arrogant smiles, so in control
Middle-aged middlemen with long faces grumbled:
"There are holes in our pockets!"
Scared of the mice they asked:
"What do we do now?"
"Where do we go from here?"
Ambitious young men with concealed smiles
replied: "Just follow the exit signs"

Soon they realized the gaps
"How do we do this – how do we do that?
Perhaps we should have stopped them?"
lacking experience, they became confused

Double-clicking with my fingertips
I glanced at the screen and saved what I had typed
"A mouse with a human brain!"
What a large trap

[Reflections on computer automation and the economic recession of the 1980's]

Time Theft

With a click of my fingertip it begins
personal photos, twenty or thirty
why not two or three?
Loved ones eager to share messages electronic
articles I mustn't miss
how can I delete without perusing
That's how it really begins

One by one I start opening all those Forwards
lest I miss the most critical of all
perusing, retaining, deleting
That's how it really begins

The daily deliveries door to door
of free newspapers
bombardment of magazines, colourful flyers
how many can I possibly read in a day
what headlines should I ignore?
Such valuable time spent
discarding, disregarding
That's how it really begins

Time I could have spent
reading by choice
creating by instinct
listening to my favourite lyrics
or simply being lost
in my *own* fantasy world

It's not just a theft of personal time
but that of cyberspace
of healthy environment too
How will it end?

Cap Language

With love to my father

What a variety of caps my father has:
The quilted round
embroidered with brown
he wears when he prays
humble and subdued
pure and pious
a glimpse of his inner beauty I'm able to catch
That woollen black one
round underneath
flat on top, tilted to the side
when he wears it,
portrays his self-confidence
sturdy and strong
willing to withstand challenges
weather the weather

The grey beret he chooses
when he feels weak and cold
helplessly aging, vulnerably gazing into space
minute by minute I see him grow old
I watch him walk, observe him talk
my father's caps communicate with me too

And now ...
oceans apart
he resides in my heart
fond memories of him I recall
his shining green eyes
pure white beard, caressing his rosy cheeks
affectionate smile

Of all the caps he wore
the black one I liked the best
for I choose to remember him as
"forever strong"
That tilt I recall
brought out his jovial side
and filled my heart with love

I pray that he remains surrounded
with his colourful roses
eternal joy, here
and in the hereafter

my father's caps communicate with me too

Hyphenated Canadian

Only after it slipped into my description
did I become fully aware of
my fresh identity
At times I question
if it's a welcome addition or not

On one hand, it's inclined to expand my personality
on the other, it seems to subtract
but why?

No matter how loyal I become
never will I be *permanently* perceived as
just a "Canadian"

What confuses me is the order
in which should fall these two terms
What should come before the hyphen
what should fall after?

Am I a Canadian-Pakistani, or a Pakistani-Canadian?
It bothers me to know
if I win a medal or achieve a miracle
I will be regarded as an accomplished Canadian
my origin will suddenly be shoved aside
if I cross a line or make a mistake
I will be regarded as a mischievous Pakistani
pushed back to where I once belonged

No harm dreaming about the ideal world
in which the hyphen doesn't dictate what I should be
instead it adds to what I already was
doesn't take away
the precious gems I've brought along
but adds to the jewels I'll now purchase
as a hyphenated Canadian

The Misery of Misrata

From a deserted desert rose
an ordinary man in a mighty robe
Hungry for power, thirsty for thrills
intoxicated he became guzzling gasoline
devouring whomever crossed his path
By the minute he grew stronger
by the hour he became taller
a normal human
turned into a demon
His giant steps crushed the ordinary
his iron fist with a twist
conquered all
Mini-demons he created to join the ranks
Full control they managed to gain
definition of progress remained
prosperity for few, poverty for most

After decades of suppression
the innocent suffered in silence
though the lips remained sealed, minds were mindful
desert storm was dangerously brewing

Tens and twenties multiplied into hundreds
hundreds into thousands soon became millions
voices previously unheard, now shouting in chorus
surging insurgents
raising arms
Exploitation ... or help?
The skies started roaring
under the order of
the most powerful being on earth

The eagles turned into fighter jets
sales of the Sky Hawks soon to boom

then began bombing and shelling
rockets and grenades – fierce battles
women raped, kids kidnapped
homes demolished
One by one cities under siege
the Misery of Misrata mounted by the hour
precious lives lost
dignity of a nation at stake
the demon had lost his eyesight
foresight of a human he no longer possessed

The day arrived
the world desperately waited
when the demon could be downed
he finally shrunk back
into an ordinary human being again

After causing so much Misery to Misrata
himself miserable
vulnerable – he remained stubborn
yet would not beg for mercy
His last chance to become a hero for some
thus lost
If only he could devour one more being
If only he could cause some more misery

"Is it really him"?
"No, it can't be him"
"Yes it is him!"
Soon the demon lay, mutilated
only the human in him remained 'inhuman'
Blood stains shall now stain
the pages of history
about Misrata's Misery

Sparkling Space

What power bestowed
to my fingertips and yours
In seconds able to 'excavate'
positive words out of space
with ability to instantly alter
my entire world to a brighter place
First they caressed my eager eyes
then travelled on to gently stroke my heart
how sombre mood
shifted to ecstatic

Invisible highways with multiple lanes
intricate traffic jams, out of control
If the entire communication in cyberspace
suddenly solidified, became visible
we would see raging Red Lights
and Amber alerts in ample "forwards"

So let us do away with
damaging communications
spread of hatred
Smooth-line the traffic
with messages of love, such as yours
touch the heart of our space
with grace
until it sparkles

In Worship

My flaws I criticize
and analyze every day
in order to remain humble
lest I cave in to narcissism

My plusses I attribute to Nature
the Creator
Regardless of criticism
a bit of narcissism
is not just my struggle for survival
but also a form of worship

Silence is Ticking

Tick ...
Tick ...
Tick ...
Tick ...
in the silence of the night
I can hear the sound of constant reminder
loud and clear
Except for the presence of another being
lying beside me in a state of neither life, nor death
yet another stark reminder
tick, tick, tick

Each moment taking us
further from the time of arrival
closer to the time of departure
I can feel the moments slipping, yet multiplying
hundreds into thousands
uncountable

How many were spent in pleasures
how many in pressures of life?
How many were seized
and how many let go?

Tick, tick
... the dividing line between life and death
is but a series of ticks
gaining momentum by the minute;
tick, tick, tick, tick, tick ...
and then ...
... silence

Suhaag Raath

(Wedding night)

The parents confidently declare:
"Love marriages western style, often fall apart
The well-being of our child, we know best"
No ifs, ands or buts
the package will soon be ready –
to be sealed, signed, and delivered
Love by Arrangement

Festivities begin with *dholkees* –
dancing and singing parties
then the festive *henna* ceremony
Preparations with mixed emotions
anticipation for *Suhaag Raath* – the honeymoon night
In advance the bride is 'pampered to death'
body massages with delicate herbs
adding to the aroma of anticipated love
mehndi mix wrapped in silver cones
to decorate her tender hands and feet
with floral designs

Finally the day approaches
when she signs her life
into the hands of a total stranger
As usual the parents boast:
"Oh but it is she who first gives her consent"
Consent?
Succumbed to her upbringing, she remains silent
Amidst tears of joy and sorrow she departs
the *baraath* proudly takes the bride away

Her bed surrounded with garlands
of jasmine and marigolds

Dressed in red *Lehnga* – a colour to depict happiness –
the colour of roses, she herself is but a rose
beauty encompassed by innocence
delicate as a petal

The Prince majestically makes his grand entrance
clad in white *Sherwaani*, wearing a gleaming smile
She too responds, beaming with innocence
genuine, or maybe fake? No one knows
intoxicated with victory, he's delighted nonetheless

Slowly he moves
one by one he removes
her dangling earrings
heavy gold necklace down to her cleavage
he tries to caress with his fingertips
Bells are ringing,
alarms too – on the inside

Her glass bangles create music of romance
that excites him even more
he opens her decorated palms to caress
ah, that sweet aroma of *henna*

Rings from each of her fingers he removes
one by one
attempts to unzip her blouse
Never before touched by a male
she shies away, signals him she'll do it herself

Discreetly, swiftly
slips into her negligee
still trying to conceal her stunning curves
a source of pride and joy but
'modesty' long preached

As she's just beginning to
get over her apprehensions
the desire paves its way
before she's fully excited
he's already dressing up!

She lays there lethargic, wondering:
Will it also be like this in other aspects of life?
Is this what marriage means?
Donating myself to life 'for life'?

Surface the two phrases long instilled in her mind:
A daughter leaves her parents' home
only with the Baraath and ...
her husband's home
only in her Janaazah [funeral]

Will he love me, respect my desires?
Would we eventually learn
to *love* each other?

*As she's just beginning to
get over her apprehensions ...
he's already dressing up!*

Meditation

Along with a deep breath
inhale your mind's power to its fullest
hold it there for as long as possible

Gently exhale your vulnerability
in its entirety
repeat the motion time after time
in steady rhythm
let go of gravity
Feels good to disconnect
with the material world altogether
your imagination will help you finally take off
hold on to it tightly

The transition might challenge you
relax completely to achieve weightlessness
when your eyelids feel heavy
it's a positive sign
bear with it
this could well be your entry point

Once the pain diminishes
you've finally entered a constellation
you are now a sparkling particle in the universe
floating gently
adding to its serenity

The mundane no longer exists

Tahrir Square

The face of the Sphinx, sad and disfigured
its tears flowing into the Nile along with mine
I watch in suspense
the pyramid of power about to collapse
danger lingers
blue waters might turn red any time
What a dramatic standoff
a match forty years in the making
liberty versus autocracy
Glued to my sixty-inch square box
in apprehension I switch channels

The voice of justice once unified
on the seventh day is easily muffled
by the surprise roar of camels and wild horses
Motherland helplessly watches
as siblings squabble
Gaining momentum
peaceful demonstrations turn to dreadful destruction
"Oh God let it not be another Tiananmen Square
let Tahrir be true *Tahrir*"
The right is wrong
but the wrong is always right
it's been proven time after time
so why do we bother to fight?
We cannot let the bricks fall
so the answer is "No"
they are disappointed and depressed
so am I

As the wind of frustration sweeps
across North Africa
from west to east

the defining moment must arrive
or the architects of revolution emotionally charged
will continue to sleep on the streets

Right is this fight for their rights
by the everyday Egyptians, I feel so proud ... but
will their empty hands declare victory?

Six thousand years of history
pages turning at a blinding pace
it's not just eighteen days of perseverance;
it's thirty years of patience
Eyes looking upwards, ears attentive
the whole world watches
The long awaited announcement is finally made
a big brick has fallen
the modern pharaoh is removed

Fireworks of jubilation
Facebook Revolution, grassroots movement
whatever you may call it
I'm as jubilant as the crowd I watch

Uniforms, under the banner of ephemerality
now hold the sceptre
with scepticism I share the emotions of ecstasy
but what next?
Will the crowd raise arms
in Tahrir Square once again?

Grandma's Green Room

Grandma's green room converted
into the grandkids' playroom
Adorned with toys, teddy bears and dancing dolls
it now spells "innocence and fun"
affection
Grandchildren are away today
so loneliness may find its own way
Grandma is about to discover a magical toy
that casts eternal joy:

After days of cloudy weather
today brilliant sunshine boldly filters
through the vertical blinds of my green room
lights up the faces of dolls
animals play merrily too
I put down my Earl Grey and
recline on this comfy couch
now used by my grandchildren

It still has a spot for me
though they now call *me* their "comfy couch"
whenever I cuddle them on my lap
Spontaneously I remove my lounging gown
the sun rays mingled with the green
how they play on my skin
the ultra violet rays;
tan limbs magically turn violet blue
a rainbow is in the making too

I close my eyes
and hear silence that previously eluded me
feel only the warmth of the sun on my skin
So this is the Grandma's toy, I think
untouchable, yet so adorable

Once the curtains of my eyelids drawn down,
a bright red canvas appears inside
painting pictures of pleasures with the kids
I feel joy
my eyes closed, a smile splashed
I turn my face towards the hallway
strangely I discover
the inner canvas suddenly turns black
how colours range from dark to light
yellow to orange and various hues

Back and forth I experiment, flirting with light
This little ten by ten cubicle painted dark green
a laboratory for experiment
it was never meant to be
just a playroom for Grandma

Playing with the Eternal Toy, our joy
how swiftly the hour passes by

Then, the all-too-familiar chime of the dryer
reaches her ears
playtime is over
but before she exits the room
she winds the musical doll

Comfort Zone

Part of you is who you really are
but a part of you is perhaps my own perception
through the lens of my heart
that may well be prone to misinterpretation
Whether it's a matter of idealizing, or idolizing
why prove it wrong?

Continue to hold my hand gently
whisper softly, stroll slowly
Let's not get carried away towards a destination
from where the only option left
is to retreat
I thrive in my comfort zone
don't you?

Rendezvous

As though cautious of disturbing her sleep
sensing her silent breath
gently I stepped back
overheard her family whisper:
"Why did you dress Grandma in green?
She always wore black
Why did you leave her hair free,
instead of her usual braids?"

To me she looked like a doll, in her eighties
"But Mom,
Grandma did want her long silver hair to be left loose
she wanted to wear the green two-piece suit
That's how she had dressed when
she met Grandpa for the first time"

The visit to her beloved so well planned
her firm conviction
she would meet him again

Upon reflection it became clear
she had wanted to step back in time
and be young for her lover again
choice of green to represent youth?

Her soul has left
only the body remains for now but ...
soon it shall perish and
the soul will live on
I wiped my tears and smiled
After forty years of separation
she has finally joined her beloved
Why grieve?
time to celebrate their "Rendezvous"

In Tune

My precise perception
of my taste for tunes
Abstract is this yearly gift of love
from my nephews and nieces

Upon my arrival they commence
selecting special songs
keeping in mind
which latest tunes I'd like best
what lyrics would caress my finer senses

Prior to my departure and goodbye
music with ambiance – a listening session they arrange
Under the dim lights I secretly observe
delicate expressions on their serene faces
stealthily glancing at mine
rejoicing, wondering, confirming
if their choices were right

How they preserve so much love
into such a compact disc
Upon return to Canada I play over and over
relive and relish those moments
Though I reside thousands of miles away
so accurate is their perception
of my taste for music – abstract love

Together or apart
we're always in tune

Self-Proclaimed

With heads and faces covered
they may boast all they want
unaware of harsh realities
Stark naked in fact they stand at the podiums
professing piety
exposing decades of ignorance
centuries of slumber
pronouncing judgments upon others
claiming custody of hell and heaven

Their notes have long been lost
glorious past now history

Who can make them realize
their tactics will only elicit
further ridicule
greater exploitation?

A Craving

Against the sky neither blue nor black
mysterious majestic trees
unidentifiable colours
I witnessed darkness
secretly embracing the daylight
silence soothed, air was pure
birds started singing *chanson d'amour*
harmony touched my soul
If only
I could seize the moment

Slowly waking up from deep sleep
in minutes, shades of green
focused
lines, shapes, clearly defined
colours of flowers
distinct
the night had finally kissed goodbye

A raging police car
tore across the silken fabric of peace
fuel and fume, smog and smoke
speeding trains and uptight ambulances
peace and tranquillity drowned
in an ocean of disruption
time to get ready for work

How I long for another dawn
to come closer yet again
to the Creator

Surfing with Caution

Surfing is your favourite sport
you enjoy playing with the high tide
Afraid of the deep seas
I prefer to watch from a distance
surfing the sandy beaches instead
My sixth sense, with the reputation of precision
predicts if I plunge into the ocean
for lack of skills, I could be doomed

As you enjoy the rise and fall
of each and every tide, surging on the inside
I willingly curb the desire and admire
but when a large wave playfully hits the sea shore
I love walking on wet sand
as I feel the ground move from under my feet
with pleasure I waver
until the waters have fully receded

Oh! Here comes that fascinating surge again
what a huge swirl
Casting the surfboard with confidence
just as you get excited with each ominous onslaught
I too look forward to sprinkles that tickle
barely get my feet wet
I splurge and splash in my own pleasures
safe and sound
on my own ground

I splurge and splash in my own pleasures
safe and sound
on my own ground

Smiling Maids

Slender, fragile females
have scattered themselves
all over the world
Smiling faces, soft spoken
selflessly they toil all day long
sparkling sinks, shining floors, many other chores

To affluent strangers
such physical comfort they provide
What about emotional comfort of their own?
Beneath those misleading smiles
are aching hearts and troubled minds
sad stories of alienations, separations

While one offspring may be in the Philippines
with grandparents
another could be left in India with the in-laws
the spouse, perhaps labouring hard
in yet another part of our world
may have come to Canada via Israel
or at the courtesy of another country

Only through cyber-technology
they remain connected
their families longing to be re-united
Tirelessly continue to labour, counting days
waiting for that special eight and a half by eleven
about which dreams half the third world

Do we even realize the price they pay
the Filipino maids
to become hyphenated Canadians?

A Puff of Cool Breeze

Sitting on the doorsteps of my house
contemplating *'life'*
on a hot summer afternoon
I was fatigued
when like a puff of cool breeze
in the heat of the moment
you passed by

Centuries had elapsed since we met
we barely even knew each other
neither you nor I had ever exchanged a single word
You suddenly surfaced, along with
a memory you once consciously captured
unconsciously I had preserved

Now that you have reappeared in my life
those magical moments we managed to seize
counted on fingertips
You shared your pains with such ease
the tragic loss of your sister
comfortably spoke of blessings too
found in an untried life philosophy

How we bonded over stories of bravery
challenges that both of us faced
You talked about the next life
I spoke of the past
a familiarity now vaguely unfamiliar
wishful thinking, we were joking

A song we shared
a poem we exchanged
the music you've gifted me since
has struck such a cord

a lifetime of conversation in person
may not convey as much
as is beautifully expressed
in these simple lyrics and intricate tunes

Our paths may never cross again
in reincarnation, I do not believe
here and now is important
as I replay those tunes
again and again
reliving
in the heat of the moment
a puff of cool breeze
that passed me by
gently

Eulogized

With heavy hearts and hefty shovels
they performed the rituals
of being the first
to pour dirt over me
pay tribute in tears and prayers
before the major task was left to a bulldozer

Once covered with a heap of mud
all other mudslinging stopped too

After burying me deep
my eulogy, they read aloud
how swift was the conversion of perception?
Sarcasm transformed into sweetness
criticism to compliments
flaws forgotten, jealousies vanished
praises that would make me so proud
The hands with which they pointed fingers
were now willing to salute me instead

Having become such a hero
swellhead, I tossed and turned inside my grave
with a deadly desire
to relive this life once again

Reluctant,
I then shuddered with the thought;
will their opinions instantly revert?
Perhaps I'm better dead than alive
eulogized, I'm so purified

Attention Span

Circles of light upon the ceiling
one constantly moving
narrowing, expanding, then rotating
the other two still, silently watching

Immersed in the sunlight and sitar melody
attention travelled
away from the sound, onto the light
two circles remained intact but
the third one suddenly ceased to move
no longer expanding or contracting

Resting upon the table it was my own foot
which had now stopped dancing
A cloud moved in
and all circles disappeared

Wasn't it the light of the Creator?

Eclipse

Faces formed of fearful flesh
arms turned into magnets
Like vultures they hover around trash
seeing heaps of garbage, eyes sparkle
a gold mine they've finally found
Digging deep into the waste the magnets attract
rusty screws, twisted nails, discarded bottle tops
empty cans to be converted into coins
Another soft hand
stealthily pierces through the mush
of stale *curry and daal*
luckily lands onto a drumstick half eaten
eyes suddenly shine with hope
a lamb chop with left over fat around the bone
a rotten peach partially eaten, good for desert
a feast is finally in sight!

The nation's child gladly sits on a heap of garbage
oblivious
that behind him on the horizon
the sun is shining bright upon the fortunate few
his silhouette dark, and his future
in total eclipse

Saree Shopping

In those narrow alleys
of Karachi's Bohri Bazaar and Zainab Market
and on the unpaved streets
of Rawalpindi's Mauthee Bazaar and Gakkhar Plaza
Where the South Asian population density
announces itself, along with loud horns
Where the disparity
between the haves and the have-not's
boldly stares you in the face
I was feeling
     and behaving
          like a foreigner
I had become a Canadian!

A million eyes were staring at me
as I fumbled my way through
clumsily attempting to avoid the potholes
trying to latch on to my father's hand
walking behind him like a little girl
excited, intimidated
he was taking me shopping

Boys under ten followed us
trying to sell elastics, hair pins, *kamarbands*
Though my family drags me to shop
at the air-conditioned Park Tower in Karachi and
Jinnah Super in Islamabad,
how can I ever forget
that unique experience of my *saree* shopping?

What a treasure island of precious collections
glitter and glow instantly bedazzled me so
different from the Eaton Centre of Toronto

From vibrant fabrics of home grown cotton
to hand-woven pure silks with intricate designs
by the artisans of Pakistan
Amazing talents busy at work
in those little cubicles, the gold mines

'If only they exported half of it,
the country might not be as poor, perhaps'
naïve thought flashes through my mind

As we entered each shop
young boys were ordered by older men:
"Oeye, Chautay!
Saab te Begum Saab de waastay thanda jaa Fanta laa"
Salesmanship at its best, cold drinks ordered
pedestal fans instantly turned on

To prevent my hair
from blowing off my skull altogether,
I covered my head with my flimsy chiffon *dupatta*
Instantly blended in with the locals
a sense of relief

Another slender young boy
hopped over a tall wooden stool
started modelling glamorous *saree* after *saree* for us
how swiftly he pleated each six yards of fabric
between his forefinger and his thumb
After twenty years of experience I felt like a novice
He firmly tucked in the pleats around his waist
and wiggled a little
spread out the embroidered *palloo* on his left arm,
tilted his neck with joyful pride, a perfect model
the wobbly stool his risky catwalk!
I tried to replace his masculine face with mine
"Oh, I like this one. *Ouf Allah*, look at that one
so exclusive!"

I was falling for every second item presented
yet he continued to fuss
His firstborn pet child
being pampered with a special treat
patient in anticipation

I liked one so much I declared:
"This is it *Abbajee*. My heart is dead-set on this one"
"Too much glitz for your mother's exquisite taste"
"Ah, so this isn't for me?"
Surprised, shocked, disappointed, excited –
talk about mixed emotions, I felt them all
"Don't you know? It's our 45th anniversary?"

We brought home a classy masterpiece, a surprise
that six yards of silk in grey
delicately embroidered with dusty rose
I never will forget that evening
how he stood in the doorway
as I helped my mom dress up
His smiling green eyes sparkling with admiration
love radiating from him
Stunningly beautiful, she cast her magic smile his way
"My Mona Lisa," he said
A compliment to her, joy for me

[Part II continued on page 116]

Salim

Stunningly beautiful, she cast her magic smile his way
"My Mona Lisa," he said
A compliment to her, joy for me

II. *[Saree Shopping continued]*

Six decades of adoration sadly came to an end

Frail with age, she now watches him smile at her
from the photo on the wall – which we once snapped
of him as he clapped over a sixer
while watching cricket on TV

How she gently strokes
the empty side of that king-size bed
upon which they always lay, holding hands

Both her hands suddenly clasped
She saw me smile at her smile
"Remember my grey silk *saree*?" she asked

"How can I forget that, *Ammee?*"
Twenty years seemed just yesterday

"Your father asked me to gift it to you"
I reached out to kiss ...
his Mona Lisa

Sound of Music

Without our ability to hear
sounds mean nothing
How vast is this realm
sound of soothing music to the sound of loud sirens
soft whispers, harsh hollers
gentle breeze, roaring thunders
chirping birds and howling hyenas
roaring engines, clicking, tapping or knocking
noises and voices we hear all day long

A special sound maybe invoked
only by imagination
heightened awareness
concentration at will
If you're able to tap into the latent
block all other sounds
focus upon the passing of each moment
movements around the orbits
the electro-magnetic fields
slowly it becomes audible –
the one *constant* sound
we unconsciously seem to ignore
perhaps that's the sound of our universe

Only the lucky may tune in

A Special Connection

Neither in love nor in lust
It is not just a "meeting of the minds" either
even the term *platonic* does not describe it well
A part of my heart that has a *mind*
seems to have connected
to your mind that has a *heart*
Such a complicated connection
how do we dismantle and why?

Your absence did not make
my heart grow fonder
but when you were away I realized
if circumstances were to separate us for good
fond memories would take over ... but
If you wilfully abandon your special spot
who will suffer the greater loss?

Such a unique friendship
why can't we just celebrate?
Together ...
or even apart

Salon Poetry

To Frank

The poet in me identifies with him
observes similarity
One after the other, he beautifies
young women, old women, pretty girls,
boys of various hues and heights
Trimming long hair to short
turning straight hair into swirls
straightening out natural curls
transforming brunettes to brilliant blondes
blondes to brunettes
women's vanity and whims
his own work of art he so enjoys
Isn't it what poetry is all about?

Trimming a life story into a poem
turning experiences into metaphors and imagery
straightening out the curls
of contradictions in characters
transforming ordinary people into celebrities
celebrities into ordinary people

A poet's whims – my own work of art I so enjoy
creativity and vanity
simultaneously at play today

Frank and I go back a few decades when
he first catered to my whim
transformed my eastern looks into western
I now live far ... but
something keeps bringing me back
to good old Frank
We share stories and jokes, poetry too

we laugh, we brag
and sometimes even nag

From under the hair dryer
at times I observe him in deep discussion
with female strangers, not so strange to him
It sounds like therapy
intimate details they share
like long-time friends

Today is taking a toll
they've overbooked him
He forgets this and forgets that, but
no matter what, something brings me back
to good old Frank

Confidently he brags
Anyone I touch has feelings for me
then says to me
You're a people's poet,
I dare you to write a poem about me
Jokingly, he dared ... but
little did he know my best friend is with me

So, here I am with my nifty Netbook
with colour and chemicals in my hair
I look nothing like myself
amused with my own reflection in the mirror
Word after word, I describe
this handsome Italian in his early fifties
with contrasting shirt and pants
trimming someone's hair
I too start trimming
a life story into a poem
and I know
once Frank has trimmed, curled, and blow-dried
I too will leave this place, transformed
"Your poem is ready Frank"

Inner World

Fatigued by the speed of the outer
an inner world I've created for myself
Gentle pace, soft rhythm
candlelight serene

Green and blue in complete harmony
inclined to balance each other
A rainbow appears now and then
music merges with the inner soul
spiritual sophistication
soft words aromatic
love of nature prevails

When you knocked
as an exception, I opened the door
for you to enter my fantasy world
with unspoken promises, together we tuned in
to the song of nature

Basic concept I conceived you perceived ... but
you couldn't fully grasp and absorb
nor did you like soft colours
In my lyrics, errors you captured,
the emotions you missed

Constantly summoned by the outer glitter
answer your call
please put down your brush
I'll gladly complete the picture on my own
join the outer rhythm which suits you better
let me retain my own poetry
now and then
I promise to step outside to greet you

When the moon casts its reflection
upon the silent lake
I'll be able to see
a smiling face playfully create ripples
In love with Nature
I prefer to remain here
alone at home

In love with Nature
I prefer to remain here
alone at home

Sixty-something

Heads no longer turn for a second glance
no more sparkle in their eyes as I walk by
my hormones finally blocked their points of view

Thinking about a rosebud
I was envious ... but
were I to exchange my years for youth again
I'd have to part with wisdom
experience too

At that thought, I pulled up my comforter
and fell asleep

The Thriller

The entire world engrossed in pleasure
his every move a thriller
endless energy, an outburst of art
instantly he stole his spectators' hearts
Oblivious to the suffering of his mysterious soul
they screamed, they cheered, they applauded
the agony remained concealed

Dancing body damaging soul

It's the world without spectators
free from harmful substances
which could have given him true happiness
What bigger irony –
just when he finally found peace
in everlasting slumber
the global village burst into tears

His admirers learned the hard way
Through memories and
his every move copied
by Bollywood stars
and others around the world

Michael was destined to live forever
What a Thriller

Interacting Intellect

To the intellectuals naturally drawn,
I wish to drink from their well of knowledge

Lured by one such clan
my inquisitive nature drew me closer

Kind intellect a powerful magnet
in their field of champions just a rookie
nothing new about me they revealed
instantly labelled me as "ignoramus"

But "Empathy"
a word missing from their dictionary

They failed to realize
that they had tested me
with a broken bat and busted ball

Superficially patting me on the back
in a condescending manner
led me all the way to the exit door

A player with great potential perhaps?
How could the "intellectuals" fail to recognize
oust me from the field, just like that?

With some exposure
perhaps I could surprise them
surpass all expectations
take their winning team to a higher level

Altered is my definition
"Pseudo" has been added

The hurt turned me inwards
to look at *my* darker side:
Have I not been guilty of the same
neglected those who have long extended
genuine friendships?
They may not qualify as 'intellectuals'
intelligence with humility they possess
I must turn to them with a warm shoulder
humbled

Still, having to abandon
those I'm naturally drawn to
makes me sad
I continue to search
other wells of knowledge
to quench my thirst
Libraries rich, within reach
shelves are wells ... but
will the sadness submerge?

The Listening Mind

Curious to explore this gadget
I've carried with me for decades
obeying it, my every nerve
each limb at its service ... but
the soul at times fails to conquer this rebel

Desire's momentum peaked, I embarked
from the consciousness of the "outer"
invited the "inner consciousness"
an attempt to restructure my brain
find the observer in it
True awareness, not a simple task

To receive this special guest
I meditated first
to clear the clutter, avoid disturbance
tap into latent potential
conscious awareness of the inner
Could I possibly cultivate the real I?
abandon my habitual thoughts
away from the routine and mundane?

I became excited
as the listening mind finally arrived
a window opened
a special connection
No longer nominally awake
more alert, refreshed
I finally found a listening partner
observing, critiquing, even counselling me

Such a boost to my energy
shifting from passive to active

creative inspiration arrived too
spontaneously, I picked up my pen
to share it with you

When will I be inspired next?
In anticipation, I remain sceptical
Will I let myself keep falling
into the trap of the outer
or develop the knack to summon at will
my *listening mind*

Two Statesmen

Dignity and honour
wrapped in red and white stripes
a star amongst stars
A nation once divided
in opinion and perception
now unanimous in conclusion
Saying goodbye with gun salutes
as their history completes another chapter

In stark contrast
the defeat and defiance of that rugged face

As the noose tightens
angry slurs and slogans
one more life terminated with a sigh of relief
        about
                him
                        a nation once united
now divided, in disarray
turmoil and turbulence

What a contrast in the manner
in which two statesmen were bid farewell
Democracy or dictatorship
Dignity or disgrace
Organization or anarchy
Education or lack of it

Were those the only causes
of such contrasting ends?
Was manipulation part of the big picture too?

[To Gerald Ford and Saddam Hussain]

What a contrast in the manner
in which two statesmen were bid farewell

Vertigo Philosophy

To Lilly

My heart was racing
the world around me spinning
screaming with fear I woke up to a harsh reality
the floor was up, the ceiling down
my gut in a twirl, I lay scared in a swirl

When do we take the trouble to learn
about the intricate mechanisms in our body
       and mind?

As though my ship were engulfed in a storm
nauseated, I wobbled my way
from bedroom to kitchen
inner ear gadgets I took for granted
ears weren't meant for hearing alone
Seemingly insignificant particles
mysteriously floating in minute canals
balancing my body day in and day out
keeping me from falling flat thus far
A mere virus
freedom to float disrupted
       vertigo gripped

Holding onto the railing I reflected:
the ability is taken away, so I appreciate
nature's back-up system
on my fingertips I now marvel
as one ear out of function
the other swiftly comes to rescue and
       I may balance again

So, what about the "emotional vertigo"?
positive thoughts
floating in the mysterious veins of the mind
with which to counter-act the negative
A lesson learned the hard way

Under The Rubble

The Kashmir Earthquake of 2005

For those of you who have suddenly departed
we mourn
Upon reflection we conclude
decades of poverty and neglect
you may have escaped

Disputes you knew nothing about
might have injured you after all
Sad as it may seem, your bodies now rest in peace
for those of you left behind
with crushed bodies and wounded minds
helplessly gazing into rugged spaces
Scattered pencils and books
uniforms once blue and white
now splashed with red ink

Absent from our conscious minds
the awareness of your very existence
amidst those peaks and valleys remote
Forgive us
for we remain entangled in our own lives
struggling to meet unavoidable demands

Now that the seven-point-six has jolted us all
sudden awakening
of our hearts and minds has occurred
We rush to rescue you
from under the rubble we hear you scream
your eyes filled with dust and debris
yet we see a spark of hope
as you struggle to survive

Here we come, hang onto this rope as we pull you out
here you are, safe and sound
We are so proud!

For those of you who still shiver
on the foothills of the Himalayas
perhaps the worst is yet to come

Loaves of bread we drop from above
bundles of blankets we supply
only the strongest will grab, we know
Those with wounded bodies
will give up once again
wait for the next helicopter sound
or
no sound at all

A Wailing Womb

To Anjum and Kaleem

What an ideal day for a skiing trip
rolling hills covered with
fluffy white blanket of freshly fallen snow
rows of majestic pines caressed the deep blue sky
carefree teenagers' lively laughter
blowing steam, flirting with fresh cool breeze
anticipating an exciting dive
downhill slide in groups of four
oh what fun were slinky skis
thrill in their voices mingled with anxiety too

At home, I prepared my son's favourite meal
crispy fried chicken and baked potatoes
he'd be hungry when he returned
He had just turned fourteen

The ominous sound of the doorbell
I screamed with pain
held him in my hands, my broken doll
limbs crushed, eyes closed – inside I died
Vague words, painful noises pounded my head
A truck had passed by they said
and crushed the tender teen into silence
No one steering – the driver on the floor of his truck
his body on the accelerator
empty bottle of whisky in hand
his momentary pleasure, my lifetime sorrow

Soon he is bailed out of jail
making guiltless visits to the liquor store
Where's the remedy for my pain?

Celebrating Grandmothers

Happy as a lark
sometimes I'm just a sorrow sparrow
It's that bird's eye view in my heart that's a killer
Contrasts I observe that disturb;
while in the North West
the sun may be shining bright
in the South East is an ominous dark cloud
constantly lurking

Amidst the clink of *Royal Doulton*
over high tea they relax on a patio –
the Grandmothers of North America
sipping Earl Grey and Jasmine Delight
boasting about their heavenly gifts
ecstatic at the sight of smiling innocence
they describe the warm cuddles of grandchildren
Like fresh petals, beauty unscathed
by the roughness of life

Each Grandma outdoes the other
The first word Jason spoke, or ...
when Amanda learned to crawl

How fortunate as grandmothers we all are;
while our children must deal
with dirty diapers, backpacks, cribs and strollers,
boxes of books and tons of toys,
we finally get to relax
for these are our golden years

No longer engrossed in mashing potatoes
preparing formulas
we deserve to have the luxury of this pleasure
at our leisure

One of them adds:
We do extend our helping hands ... but
enjoyment has become our rightful blessing
Play with them
then hand them over to their parents
After all we're the modern grandmas
we need time for our weekly pampering at the salon

Celebration continues:
I say, whatever time we spend with our grandchildren
should be appreciated
So, here's a toast to all of us Grandmothers
With confidence she proposes a toast

Everyone cheers ... but
one becomes sad, and sorrowful
Her throat choking she dares stand up to say:
Do you know who we should be paying the highest tribute to?

Everyone becomes attentive

Just think,
an entire generation has been wiped out
from the surface of the earth
by that monster, the deadly virus!
So, let's not forget about those Grandmothers
who have lost their offspring

Her throat chocking she continues:
Wrinkled women with aching limbs and fatigued bodies
landed with the responsibility
of raising these 'left over' children

Not to mention the burden of grief they carry
From two miles away they must fetch drinking water
for those naked orphans with potbellies

vulnerable to disease
their lives void of toys and joys

With respectful awe and awareness
everyone stands up to propose a toast and
repeat after her:

We do salute you and pray for your strength
as you are truly the Grand 'Mothers' of Africa

[Story version 'Tribute to Grand Mothers' was published in an anthology
Canadian Voices, Volume II, 2010
posted on Youtube with visual effects]

Well Wishers

"Don't just give up. Don't give in"
well-wishers' sincere advice
how it touches my heart

My best interest on their minds
such candid feedback they provide
I embrace and thank them

"Others can easily exploit and take control
your personality is too flexible"

they keep reminding:
"Don't just give up. Don't give in"
what sweet intentions

But
when it comes to my well-wishers
dealing with me themselves
a different yardstick they pick up

"Be flexible. Give in. Give up"
what a different tune they play

Once again, out of sheer love
flexible I become ... and
just "give in"

Elusive Emotion

A powerful emotion elusive
love
abstract, yet solid in the minds of many
fanned, it can become wildfire
in liquid, at its best
when flowing smoothly in both directions

Without reciprocation, lopsided ... but
only when perceived in isolation it's devastation
For those who've learned to live life to its fullest
aware of their vast universe within
it's but a fraction of the full

Yet another experience to be lived and learned
an invitation to invoke mind power
tame the ego
accepting rejection with grace
in this defeat lies one's victory
for love abounds

Once overcome
it is liberation from expectations
disappointments
This elusive emotion
even has the capacity to evaporate
leaving one to regret and wonder
if it was merely the creation
of one's own imagination

Retaliate or Evaluate

The mind counsels:

"In place of the red carpet
shards of glass they may spread
instead of rose petals,
pebbles upon you they may cast
Pangs of jealousy they feel
maybe hard for you to endure
deep-rooted insecurities in play
Basic instincts
resentment, anger from within, might surface
you may feel hurt
tempted to retaliate

Why entertain the devil's intervention?
best to stay calm
summon the angel in you instead
no need to turn the other cheek
opportunity knocks

Time for soul-searching
tame your ego
iron out your own flaws
redefine goals

Negative, turned into positive
hurt magically disappears
Smile and thank them
for they have helped you rise above"

But the heart responds:
Easier said than done

A Creative Affair

The chirping of birds
announced your arrival
another muse knocked on my door
I rose with sudden urge to outpour
my deepest emotions
a new poem the outcome
I became content to the core

To those near and dear
I willingly provide love and care
gratifying is the experience
Appreciation lacking,
a tall order it becomes
I feel fatigued

Those that I'm naturally drawn to
conditions they place
challenged by circumstances
I feel restricted

Oh, creative inspiration
in time of such need
what a delightful friend you have become
Early mornings or late nights
with each embrace you give me
I feel the ecstasy of selfless love
hoping my affair with you
will be everlasting

Oh, creative inspiration
in time of such need
what a delightful friend you have become